J B Housto
Sanford, William R.
Sam Houston : courageous
    Texas hero

$21.26
ocn768728944
09/12/2012

Sam Houston
Courageous Texas Hero

William R. Sanford and Carl R. Green

Enslow Publishers, Inc.

40 Industrial Road
Box 398
Berkeley Heights, NJ 07922
USA

http://www.enslow.com

Original edition published as *Sam Houston: Texas Hero* in 1996.

Library of Congress Cataloging-in-Publication Data

Sanford, William R. (William Reynolds), 1927–
    Sam Houston : courageous Texas hero / William R. Sanford and Carl R. Green.
        p. cm. — (Courageous heroes of the American West)
    Includes index.
    Summary: "Examines the life of Sam Houston, including his early life on the Western frontier,
his time as a soldier, leading the fight for Texas' independence, and his political career in
Texas"—Provided by publisher.
    ISBN 978-0-7660-4009-0
    1. Houston, Sam, 1793–1863—Juvenile literature. 2. Governors—Texas—Biography—Juvenile
literature. 3. Legislators—United States—Biography—Juvenile literature. 4. United States.
Congress. Senate—Biography—Juvenile literature. I. Green, Carl R. II. Title.
    F390.H84S26 2013
    976.4'04092—dc23
    [B]
                                                2011051265

Future editions:
Paperback ISBN 978-1-4644-0092-6
ePUB ISBN 978-1-4645-0999-5
PDF ISBN 978-1-4646-0999-2

Printed in the United States of America

032012 Lake Book Manufacturing, Inc., Melrose Park, IL

10 9 8 7 6 5 4 3 2 1

Illustration Credits: Enslow Publishers, Inc., p. 28; © Enslow Publishers, Inc. / Paul Daly, p. 1;
Photo by Kimberly Denny 2009, p. 12; Library of Congress Prints and Photographs, pp. 8, 15, 19,
25, 38, 41; Peter Newark American Pictures / The Bridgeman Art Library, p. 32; Shutterstock.com,
p. 43; Courtesy of Texas State Library and Archives Commission, pp. 16, 21.

Cover Illustration: © Enslow Publishers, Inc. / Paul Daly.

Contents

Authors' Note

This book tells the true story of Sam Houston. Sam was one of the American West's greatest heroes. In his day, he was known as an outstanding general and statesman. His daring exploits and fiery speeches were featured in newspapers, magazines, and dime novels. In more recent years, Sam has been the subject of novels, films, and biographies. You may find it hard to believe that one man could pack so much adventure and achievement into a single lifetime. If so, rest easy. All of the events described in this book actually happened.

Chapter 1

The Battle of San Jacinto

Weary Texans grumbled as they set up camp on the plain of San Jacinto. The date was April 21, 1836. The soldiers were tired of retreating. The Mexican army was camped almost within rifle shot. Would General Sam Houston ever let them stand and fight?

A battle had been brewing for weeks. Leading the Mexicans was General Antonio López de Santa Anna. The Mexican dictator was trying to crush the Texans' fight for independence. He had begun by marching on San Antonio. On March 6, his troops had stormed the Alamo. All of the defenders had died in that bloody battle. At Goliad, he had ordered the slaughter of almost four hundred Texan prisoners. Now only Sam Houston and his tiny army were left to defend Texas.

Tall oak trees trailed a curtain of Spanish moss over the Texans' camp. Less than a mile away, Santa

Anna's men built a barricade of brush and baggage. The dictator felt certain that the outnumbered Texans would not attack. The barricade finished, his men stacked their rifles and lay down for a siesta.

Santa Anna's confidence seemed well founded. He commanded 1,260 men to Sam Houston's 910. Sam's best hope lay in the deadeye shooting of his riflemen. He waited, hoping the Mexicans would attack.

At last, as his men grew more impatient, Sam launched an attack. First, he sent the famous scout Deaf Smith riding west to burn Vince's Bridge. With the bridge down, Santa Anna's reinforcements could not reach him. Water and marshy ground would make retreat difficult. This would be a fight to the finish.

At 3:30 P.M., Sam was ready. He mounted his white horse and led his men forward. The advancing troops flanked two small cannon called the Twin Sisters. Houston rode up and down the line. "Hold your fire, men. Hold your fire," he urged. His silent soldiers pressed forward through the tall grass. A reserve force waited in the cover of the trees.

When the sleeping enemy lay only two hundred yards away, Sam waved his hat. The Twin Sisters roared. With grapeshot in short supply, the gunners had loaded the cannon with scrap metal. Chunks of broken horseshoes ripped through the barricade. The Texans surged forward. As they ran, they yelled, "Remember the Alamo!"

Santa Anna's men groped for their guns. A few wild shots peppered the attacking Texans. Sam's white horse went down. Sam jumped free, grabbed a second horse, and swung into the saddle. A moment later, a musket ball shattered his ankle. The second horse fell under him. Somehow, Sam pulled himself onto a third horse.

The Texans broke through what was left of the barricade. Many of the Mexicans fought bravely, while others ran for their lives. Santa Anna, unnerved by the assault, fled on horseback. Eighteen minutes after the first shots were fired, the battle was over.

"¡Me no Alamo!" frightened Mexicans pleaded. The Texans were beyond caring. Blind with rage, they shot, clubbed, and knifed hundreds of helpless prisoners. When the dust settled, 630 Mexicans lay dead. Another 630 had surrendered. More than 200 of them had been wounded. Only two Texans had been killed in the surprise attack, although seven more died later of their wounds.

A patrol found Santa Anna the next day. The riders brought the dictator back to camp. They found Sam

Sam Houston, nursing his wounds under a tree, meets with Antonio López de Santa Anna after the Texans' victory at San Jacinto. General Houston offered to spare Santa Anna's life if the Mexican general promised to order his soldiers to leave Texas.

sitting under a tree, nursing his wounded ankle. Santa Anna feared he would be sent to a firing squad. Sam had a better idea. He offered to spare the dictator's life—if all Mexican troops left Texas. Santa Anna quickly signed the orders that sent his men home.

The stroke of Santa Anna's pen ended the Texas war for independence. Thanks to Sam Houston and his brave soldiers, Texas was free.

Chapter 2

Growing Up in a New Country

In 1793, the United States was still a young country. Most of its 4 million people lived near the Atlantic coast. The great surge westward was still to come.

On March 2, Elizabeth Houston of Timber Ridge plantation gave birth to her fifth son. She named the boy Samuel. The name was a tribute to her husband, Major Samuel Houston. Two days later, President George Washington began his second term.

Timber Ridge lay in a sunny valley near Lexington, Virginia. Slaves worked in the fields and helped out in the large house. Major Houston, an inspector in the state militia, was seldom home. While he was gone, Elizabeth managed the plantation. While she was busy with her duties, a slave girl took care of Sam.

Four more babies arrived over the next few years. Left free to wander the nearby woods, Sam learned to hunt, fish, and swim. When he was eight, Elizabeth sent him to a log schoolhouse. Although he often cut class, Sam mastered the arts of reading and writing. At home, his father filled his head with stories of the young nation's heroes. In his free time, the youngster read books on geography and history.

Major Houston paid his travel costs out of his own pocket. In time, his debts outstripped his income. The Houston family talked of selling out and moving west. The major's sudden death in 1807 made the move even more urgent.

Elizabeth sold Timber Ridge and bought land in eastern Tennessee. The family piled its belongings into two wagons and headed west. The grueling three-hundred-mile journey to the new farm near Maryville took three weeks. This was truly the western frontier. The Cherokee Nation owned the land on the far side of the nearby river.

Sam's older brothers carved a farm from the wilderness. Sam did his share of the work, but he was bored by farming. For a time, he went back to school. There, he fell in love with Homer's epic work, *The Iliad*. Sam never forgot those stirring tales.

Like Homer's ancient Greek heroes, he believed he was destined for greatness.

As the farm prospered, Sam's brothers invested in a dry goods store. After Sam quit school at sixteen, they put him to work as a clerk. Sam hated this job as well. When he felt too tied down, he vanished into the woods. One day, he did not return.

Weeks later, the Houstons heard that Sam was living with the Cherokee. Two of his older brothers set out to bring him home. When they reached the Indian village, they found Sam reading a book. The teenager refused to go home with them. He said he "preferred measuring deer tracks to [measuring] tape."

In time, Chief John Jolly adopted the young man. Sam, in turn, learned the tribe's language and customs. With the other young men, he played the rough ball game that later became lacrosse. He also took pride in his Cherokee name, *Co-lon-neh* (the Raven). In tribal lore, the raven was both bold and wise. To repay the Cherokee, Sam gave them powder and shot that he bought on credit.

In 1812, Sam took a job as a teacher to pay off his debts. Young Houston, the Maryville townsfolk sneered, had gone to the "Indian university." The jeers did not bother Sam. He was weak in math, but he

In 1812, Sam Houston took a job as a teacher to help pay off his debts. This is the Maryville, Tennessee, schoolhouse where Sam charged students eight dollars a term to take his classes.

knew history and geography. More to the point, he was an inspiring teacher. The price to study with Sam was high—eight dollars a term. Parents paid one-third in cash, one-third in corn, and one-third in cloth.

Years later, Sam remembered his teaching days with pride. He said he felt at that time "a higher . . . self-satisfaction than from any office or honor which I have since held." Those good feelings lasted only six months. With his debts paid, Sam went looking for a more heroic career.

Chapter 3

The Hero of
Horseshoe Bend

The War of 1812 changed Sam Houston's life forever. Once again, the former colonies found themselves at war with Great Britain. At sea, British warships forced captured American sailors to join the British navy. On land, British agents stirred up trouble with the American Indians.

Recruiters for the U.S. Army reached Maryville in March 1813. At the courthouse, an officer put a pile of silver dollars on a drumhead. Sam was one of the men who stepped forward to pick up one of the coins. With that act, the volunteers became army privates.

Twenty-year-old Sam could not enlist without his mother's consent. Elizabeth gladly gave her blessing. She also warned him, ". . . while the door of my cottage is open to brave men, it is eternally shut against cowards."

The army needed men like Sam. At six feet, three inches and 240 pounds, he towered over his fellow soldiers. Better still, this auburn-haired giant was one of the few recruits who could read and write. Within a month, Sam had risen from private to sergeant. Three months later, he won appointment as an ensign with the 39th Infantry.

In Alabama, a band of Creek Indians went on the warpath. The warriors, who carried bright red war clubs, were known as Red Sticks. On August 13, they attacked Fort Mims. Nearly five hundred settlers died in the massacre that followed.

General Andrew Jackson of Tennessee called out the militia to meet the threat. He soon found that his ill-trained troops lacked discipline. A second call went out, this time for army soldiers to help whip his men into shape. In February 1814, the 360 regulars of the 39th joined Jackson's command. Ensign Sam Houston led one of the unit's platoons.

Jackson caught up with the Creek in east-central Alabama. The Red Sticks were dug in at Horseshoe Bend on the Tallapoosa River. A double-walled barricade known as a breastworks guarded the three-hundred-acre neck of land. Muskets poked through loopholes cut into the thick walls. On March 27,

General Andrew Jackson prepares to lead his troops into battle against the Creek Indians in Alabama. Sam Houston was one of the soldiers who joined Jackson for the campaign.

Jackson's cannon opened fire on the breastworks. The stout logs held firm.

As he pondered his next move, Jackson saw black smoke rising near the river. A band of loyal Cherokee had crossed the river in canoes. Now they were torching the Creek village. Sensing that the Red Sticks were confused, Jackson ordered an assault.

The men of the 39th led the way. Major L. P. Montgomery reached the top of the wall before he was killed by a musket ball. Waving his sword, Sam led a wave of soldiers over the wall. A moment later, he went down with an arrow in his thigh.

As the fighting raged on, Sam ordered a soldier to pull out the arrow. The man tugged, but the barbed

A fellow soldier removes an arrow from Sam Houston's thigh during the battle at Horseshoe Bend. Even though he suffered several painful wounds, Sam kept on fighting. His bravery inspired his men and helped defeat the Red Sticks.

point was caught deep in the muscle. "Try again," Sam ordered. "If you fail this time, I will smite you to the earth." The man could see that Sam meant what he said. He yanked hard at the arrow. It came out in a gush of blood and torn flesh. Sam pressed a rag to the wound and hobbled off to find a doctor.

By 4:00 P.M., the last Red Sticks were holed up in a ravine. Jackson called for volunteers to storm their position. Sam picked up a musket and limped forward. A handful of men followed him. They were within five yards of the breastworks when two musket balls smashed Sam's right shoulder. His men carried him back to safety.

Jackson tried a new tactic. At his orders, a barrage of fire arrows set the Red Stick fort aflame. Marksmen cut down the last warriors as they tried to flee. The Battle of Horseshoe Bend was over.

A surgeon worked on Sam's shoulder. He quit with the job half done, certain Sam would die. To his surprise, his patient survived that pain-filled night. By morning, Sam had regained a little strength. Two months later, a horse litter carried him to his mother's house. At first, Elizabeth did not recognize him. Only the look in Sam's eyes told her this pale, gaunt figure was her son.

Chapter 4

A War Hero Runs for Office

Sam came home a hero, but the price was high. His wounds troubled him the rest of his life. By October 1814, he felt strong enough to visit Washington, D.C. There, the newly commissioned lieutenant saw the damage caused by the British raid in August. "My blood boiled" at the sight of the badly damaged buildings, Sam said later.

When the war ended in 1815, Sam remained in the army. Sent to New Orleans, the tall lieutenant with the gray-blue eyes was a welcome guest at parties. If Sam had a fault, it lay in his taste for whiskey. In fun-loving New Orleans, he had plenty of company.

By 1817, settlers were pushing onto Cherokee lands. Sam was assigned the job of persuading his Cherokee friends to move to Arkansas. When the tribe's leaders traveled to Washington for talks, Sam

During a visit to Washington, D.C., in 1814, Sam Houston witnessed the severe damage inflicted on the city during the War of 1812. This engraving shows the ruins of the U.S. Capitol after the British set fire to the building.

went with them. The Cherokee wore their splendid robes to a reception given by President Monroe. Secretary of War John C. Calhoun was outraged when Sam showed up in a tribal outfit. Because Sam had taken their side, Chief Jolly's people listened to him. They gave up their land and took the long trail west.

Sam was left with a bad feeling. Was sending his friends to Arkansas the right thing to do? In March 1818, he resigned from the army. Back in Nashville, Sam went to see Andrew Jackson and his wife. Before long, the childless Jacksons were treating Sam like a son.

With Jackson as his mentor, Sam chose the law as a career. At that time, law students studied with older lawyers. Judge James Trimble served as Sam's teacher. He told Sam to set aside a year or more to complete his law studies. The judge had not counted on his pupil's fine mind. Six months later, Sam breezed through his bar exam. His high marks gave him the right to practice law in Tennessee.

The new lawyer set up practice in the nearby town of Lebanon. In court, his deep voice and quick wit helped him win tough cases. Impressed, the county's voters picked him to be their district attorney. Sam also joined the militia, where he rose quickly in rank. In the fall of 1821, Major General Houston took command of the Tennessee state militia.

Sam took a second big step in 1823. Running unopposed, he won a seat in Congress. There he served with Henry Clay and Daniel Webster. To help the folks back home in Tennessee, he voted to build much-needed roads and canals.

Jackson made his first run for president in 1824. He came in first, but did not win a majority in the Electoral College. Lacking a clear winner, the election was thrown into the House of Representatives. Sam tried to swing Clay's support to Jackson but failed.

In 1823, Sam Houston began his political career by winning a seat in Congress. Painted in 1826, this is the earliest known portrait of the fiery soldier-politician.

Clay, who disliked Jackson, helped put John Quincy Adams in the White House. Adams, in turn, chose Clay as his secretary of state. Sam was outraged. He charged the two men with making a secret deal.

Clay and the Jackson camp next locked horns over the choice of a postmaster for Nashville. Clay wanted his son-in-law, John Erwin, to have the job. Sam, still angry, wrote a scorching note to President Adams. The note accused Erwin of having poor morals. To avenge the insult to his friend, William White challenged Sam to a duel. Sam did not back down. Given his choice of weapons, he chose pistols at fifteen paces.

On September 21, the two men met in a pasture. White shot first—and missed. Sam's return shot, however, hit White in the groin. Later, Sam said, "Thank God [White] was injured no worse."

Sam did not let the close call bother him. In 1827, he ran for governor of Tennessee. He campaigned in shiny black trousers, red sash, hunting shirt, and a beaver hat. His platform called for state support of roads and canals, schools, and trade. In a frontier state, it was a good blueprint for growth.

Sam won a two-year term as governor. A year later, in 1828, the people of the United States gave Andrew Jackson his long-sought victory. Governor Houston shared the triumph with the new president. Sam, it was whispered, might one day follow Jackson to the White House.

Chapter 5

Two Marriages

S am tried hard to be a good governor. Even so, he made enemies. Some people disliked him for treating American Indians fairly. Others hated him for his ties to Andrew Jackson. All agreed that the thirty-five-year-old bachelor drank too much.

Friends advised Sam to marry and settle down. Sam did not argue the point. He had already picked out his bride-to-be. His choice was blonde Eliza Allen. A friend described her as "not pretty, but . . . graceful, and queenly."

Eliza was in no rush to marry. Her parents, though, sided with Sam. The Allens wanted to have a governor in the family. Late in December 1828, Eliza said yes. The wedding took place a month later. Robert Allen led his twenty-year-old daughter down a wide staircase. The groom looked splendid in a cloak lined with scarlet satin. After a short honeymoon, the newlyweds moved into the Nashville Inn.

The marriage was a stormy one. Eliza hated politics. The rough talk and heavy drinking upset her. The strains increased when Sam announced he would seek a second term. In April 1829, he found Eliza crying over old love letters. A few harsh words led to too many more. Eliza charged Sam with insane jealousy. Sam, in turn, said she had never been a loving wife. That may have been true. The sight of his raw, poorly healed wounds may have sickened her.

The outburst settled nothing. Sam left town for a debate. When he returned, he found that Eliza had left him. Sam followed her to the Allen home. The Allens would not let him see Eliza alone. An old aunt kept watch when the two met. Sam knelt and begged Eliza to return. She refused.

Rumors spread that Sam had treated Eliza badly. Angry men burned a dummy dressed to look like the governor. Soldiers had to be called out to break up the mob. Sam brooded in silence for five days. Then he resigned his office. His enemies laughed, "Poor Houston, rose like a rocket and fell like a stick."

A steamboat carried Sam westward. He drank too much and thought of suicide. In that dark moment,

After Sam Houston's marriage failed, he traveled west to Arkansas to live with Chief Jolly and his people. During his stay, Sam dressed like a traditional Cherokee warrior and helped bring peace between the Cherokee, Osage, and Creek tribes.

an omen lifted his spirits. As Sam stood on deck one evening, he saw an eagle fly past. The great bird swooped low, then flew into the sunset. In that moment, Sam wrote: "I knew that a great destiny waited for me in the West."

Chief Jolly welcomed his adopted son to the tribe's Arkansas home. Sam took off his city clothes and put on Cherokee dress. Before long, he had taken on the role of peacemaker. Thanks to his efforts, the Cherokee, Osage, and Creek tribes agreed to live in peace. In October 1829, the Cherokees made him a citizen of their nation. Sam knew it was a great honor.

The Raven set up a trading post on the Arkansas River. Still depressed, he tried to drown his troubles in whiskey. Soon, the Cherokee gave him a new name— Big Drunk. In the midst of his sorrows, Sam found love again. He married Chief Jolly's niece, Tiana Rogers. Sharing a home with Tiana helped restore his will to live. As his gloom lifted, he picked up his pen. The newspaper articles he wrote called attention to the white man's abuse of the American Indians.

In 1831, Sam was called home to bury his mother. After the funeral, he met with President Jackson. Jackson asked Sam to keep him informed on affairs in Texas. At that time, Texas belonged to Mexico. The papers Jackson signed made Sam his official representative. With them, Sam could move freely through Mexican territory.

Back in Arkansas, Sam sold the trading post. He gave Tiana his house and land. Then he said good-bye and rode south. As far as Sam was concerned, the marriage was over. Late in 1832, he crossed the Red River into Texas.

Chapter 6

The Struggle for Independence

Texas was all that Sam had dreamed it would be. In an eloquent letter to his cousin, he wrote: "Texas is the finest portion of the globe that has ever blessed my vision."

In San Felipe, Sam hooked up with knife-fighter Jim Bowie. On a trip to San Antonio, the two men talked peace with the Comanche. Back in San Felipe, Sam called on Stephen F. Austin. The founder of Texas must have liked the newcomer. Sam left the meeting with the rights to a league of land—4,428.4 acres. Austin's price was $375 (eight cents an acre). Sam paid for the land with "a fine American horse."

Early in 1833, Sam opened a law office in Nacogdoches. By Mexican law, lawyers had to be Catholic. That was fine with Sam. As required, he took a saint's name. Then he talked a priest into baptizing him. At night, Samuel Paul Houston took Spanish

Sam Houston's Texas

Texas State Boundary By 1850 →

NEW MEXICO

INDIAN TERRITORY

Red River

TEXAS 1836–1848

NACOGDOCHES

Sabine River

INDEPENDENCE • • WASHINGTON-ON-THE-BRAZOS

AUSTIN •

SAN ANTONIO DE BEXAR

Rio Grande

THE ALAMO SAN JACINTO

SAN FELIPE •

GOLIAD •

COLUMBIA

Galveston Bay

HOUSTON •

MEXICO

MEXICO

EL CAMINO REAL (THE ROYAL ROAD)

GULF OF MEXICO

Sam Houston arrived in Texas late in 1832, calling it "the finest portion of the globe" he had ever seen. This map of Texas shows places that were important in Sam's life.

lessons from Anna Raguet. He fell in love, but Anna kept him at arm's length.

For Texans, life under Mexican rule was becoming harder to bear. In June 1832, blood was shed in a clash between settlers and army troops. To avoid further conflict, a convention met in April 1833 at San Felipe. Sam's neighbors sent him to speak for them. At that time, Texas was part of the state of Coahuila. The delegates voted to ask Mexico to make Texas a state in its own right. Austin carried the request to Mexico City. President Antonio López de Santa Anna, newly risen to power, turned him down.

Sam's old shoulder wound still pained him. Soaking in the mineral baths at Hot Springs, Arkansas, restored his health. When he returned, angry Texans were cursing Santa Anna. Sam counseled patience. If war broke out, he said, Mexico would win. The Texas militias would be no match for a modern army.

In 1835, a Mexican officer jailed two Texas traders. The arrest started a new round of trouble. Led by William Travis, a makeshift force of Texans freed the traders. Santa Anna sent General Martín Cós to tame the settlers. Stephen Austin called on Texans to prepare to fight. In Nacogdoches, Sam took command of the town militia. "The morning of glory is dawning upon us," he told his men. "The work of Liberty has begun."

At Gonzales, settlers guarded a small brass cannon. When a Mexican force came to seize the gun, the Texans stood firm. A volley of rifle fire forced the troops to retreat. A bigger triumph followed at San Antonio. After a short siege, General Cós surrendered the city. The easy victories did not fool Sam. The Texans had been facing troops who were poorly led and badly equipped. Battle-tested regulars would soon take over the fighting.

A new convention met at San Felipe. Still trying to avoid a fight, its leaders again asked for statehood.

Santa Anna's answer was to lead his army northward. Faced with this threat, the convention asked Sam to serve as commander-in-chief of the Texas forces. Sam said he needed five thousand men. Because the army relied on volunteers, the goal was never met. When he tried to unite his scattered forces, his orders often were ignored.

In January 1836, Sam ordered William Travis to leave the Alamo. But Travis refused. He believed the fortress could withstand a siege. In the end, the courage of the Alamo's defenders was not enough. All the Texans died during the battle on March 6 or soon afterward. At Goliad, James Fannin also ignored Sam's orders. Trapped there by Mexican troops, he was forced to surrender. Santa Anna's men shot Fannin and another four hundred prisoners on March 27.

Sam had turned forty-three on March 2, the same day Texas declared its independence. Now it was up to Sam and his men to finish the job. In the weeks that followed, he pulled back as Santa Anna advanced. His soldiers grumbled and complained. Some quit the army. At last, on April 21, Sam found a field to his liking. In the smoke and flames of San Jacinto, the Republic of Texas won its freedom.

Chapter 7

From Independence to Statehood

The war left the hero of San Jacinto with two major problems. The first involved his purse. Texas could not afford to pay Sam for his war service. The second involved his health. His wounded leg was badly inflamed.

In mid-May, Sam sailed to New Orleans for medical treatment. A crowd cheered as he limped off the boat. A moment later, he collapsed on the dock. Friends rushed him to a doctor, who cut out bone chips and rotted flesh. Afterward, Sam walked with a limp until the day he died.

That fall, Texas picked its first president. Stephen Austin and Henry Smith ran for the office. The people did not support either man. They wanted Sam Houston. Eleven days before the election, Sam bowed to the pressure. His fellow Texans rewarded him with 80 percent of their votes.

Sam Houston signed the original handwritten Texas Declaration of Independence on his forty-third birthday—March 2, 1836. Seven months later, he was sworn in as the new republic's first president.

Sam was sworn in on October 22, 1836. His government met in Columbia, the new capital. President Houston lived in a hut with dirt floors. He stuffed rags into the window frames because there was no glass. Sam and Secretary of State Austin wanted Texas to join the Union. The United States, however, had other ideas. Some Americans argued that making Texas a state would lead to war with Mexico. Abolitionists screamed even louder. They hated the thought of adding a new slave state to the Union.

In 1837, Sam divorced Eliza. Tiana had died of a fever. Single once more, he renewed his pursuit of Anna Raguet. Anna enjoyed his courtship but would not say yes to his marriage proposal. A failed romance, however, was the least of Sam's problems. Texas was a million dollars in debt. American Indian raids were on the rise. Sam had to use his own funds to help feed the army. Half of his navy was stranded in New York harbor. Texas could not pay the shipbuilding costs.

Lured by cheap rent, Sam moved the capital to Houston. The new town had been named in his honor. To cut costs, he reduced the army by two-thirds. His agents in the United States tried to sell Texas bonds, but investors were hard to find. One of Sam's pet projects did work out well. The Texas Rangers brought a measure of law and order to the frontier.

By law, Sam could not succeed himself. In the election of 1838, Mirabeau Lamar won the office. Sam detested Lamar. He took his revenge on the day Lamar was sworn in. Dressed as George Washington, Sam gave a three-hour farewell speech. The sight of Sam in his powdered wig, combined with the length of his address, left Lamar speechless.

Free from his duties, Sam went on tour to talk up the wonders of Texas. In Alabama, he met the wealthy Nancy Lea. Sam almost forgot his sales pitch when he saw the widow's violet-eyed daughter. For Margaret Lea and Sam Houston, it was love at first sight.

Back home, friends elected Sam to the state House of Representatives. By this time, the free-spending Lamar had moved the capital to Austin. Sam thought the move was wasteful. He also argued that the town was exposed to Indian attacks.

Sam, a battle-scarred forty-seven, married twenty-one-year-old Margaret Lea in May 1840. The newlyweds moved into a home on Galveston Bay. To please his bride, Sam gave up hard liquor. He also went to church more often.

In 1841, Sam won a second term as president. To set an example, he refused to live in the mansion Lamar had built. He also tried to switch the capital back to Houston. The people of Austin fought the move by standing guard over the state archives. Hotheads in the legislature gave Sam an even bigger headache. Their claims to New Mexico and California touched off a brief war with Mexico. Their southern neighbor would be a threat, Sam preached, until Texas joined the Union.

Margaret gave birth to Sam, Jr., in 1843. The proud father was soon back at work, hatching a new plan. To put pressure on the United States, he sought a treaty with Great Britain. The tactic worked. Washington did not want the British to gain a foothold in the Southwest. Three months after Sam's term ended, Congress voted to annex Texas. President John Tyler signed the bill on March 1, 1845.

Sam and Margaret set out to share the great news with Andrew Jackson. Sadly, Sam's old friend died three hours before they reached Nashville.

Chapter 8

Sam Returns to Washington

S am turned fifty-three in 1846. Margaret hoped he would retire. To her dismay, the Texas legislature chose him to be one of the state's senators. When Sam left for Washington, Margaret's poor health kept her in Texas.

In March, Sam began his two-year term. There was nothing shy about him. On the Senate floor, he wore a cougar skin waistcoat. On the street, he often threw a Mexican blanket over his shoulder.

Oregon was the chief subject of debate that year. In long, fiery speeches, Sam urged the United States to claim the entire territory. Cautious souls argued that doing so would lead to war with Great Britain. War, Sam shot back, was better than losing honor or empire. In time, cooler heads drew the northern border for the Oregon Territory at the forty-ninth parallel.

When war did break out in 1846, it was with Mexico. Sam was not surprised. Mexico and Texas, he told the Senate, had long been at war.

Margaret, lonely and often ill, missed her husband. Sam loved her, but politics was in his blood. He worked hard to win a full six-year term. His resistance to the spread of slavery hurt his campaign. Southerners called him a traitor. A slave owner himself, Sam promised he would not vote to ban slavery.

The Mexican War ended in February 1848. The peace treaty added half a million square miles to the United States. Would the western lands be free or slave? Sam still believed in the Missouri Compromise of 1820. That law had confined slavery to states below latitude 36°30'. The South cursed Sam anew when he backed the Compromise of 1850. The bill allowed the admission of California as a free state. Texans also complained about losing their claim to New Mexico. Sam told them the state gained more than it lost. One section of the bill canceled the state's old debts.

Sam often came home to find Margaret nursing a new baby. In all, the couple had eight children. After moving to Independence, Sam delighted Margaret by asking to be baptized. Despite his earlier baptism, he had never worshiped as a Catholic. That Sunday,

In 1853, Sam Houston was elected to his third term as one of his state's senators. This 1850 illustration shows the U.S. senate at work in its ornate chamber in Washington, D.C.

churchgoers were shocked to find that local kids had filled the baptismal font with mud. The prank did not let Sam off the hook. The Baptist preacher dunked his convert in the icy waters of nearby Rocky Creek.

In 1852, the Democrats thought of running Sam for president of the United States. Sam liked the idea. He was already a hero in the North. Now he tried to mend fences in the South. The right to own slaves, he said, could not be taken away. As the clear favorite, Sam thought he had earned the nomination. Party leaders did not agree. They picked Franklin Pierce.

In 1853, the people of Texas elected Sam to a third Senate term. A year later, Congress passed the controversial Kansas-Nebraska Act. New states north of 36°30' now could choose to be free or slave. The South saw the act as a chance to add new slave states. Sam, however, feared it would rip the nation apart. As much as he loved the South, he loved the Union more.

Would Kansas be slave or free? In 1856, armed bands fought for the right to make the choice. As blood flowed on the prairie, two new parties were born. The Republicans campaigned to end slavery. Sam was alarmed. Sending a Republican to the White House might force the South to secede.

The newly formed American party was pro-Union but not antislave. Sam felt at home with the secretive party, even though its members were often called the Know-Nothings. Their hatred of immigrants and Catholics did not upset him. For a time, it looked as though Sam would be the Know-Nothing candidate. In the end, the party picked former president Millard Fillmore.

Texans called Sam a traitor and worse. In 1857, two years before his term ended, the legislature picked his successor. Sam stormed back to Texas and entered the race for governor. He blasted his foes, calling them "swindlers," "forgers," and "cowards." Nothing helped. For the first time, the voters turned their backs on Sam.

Chapter 9

The Final Battles

Sam came home in March 1859 after finishing his term in the Senate. All he hoped for, he wrote, was to be with his wife and children. He said he would raise sheep and cattle on his Cedar Point farm. Margaret noted that his limp was worse.

The quiet life ended all too soon. The sight of an old foe running for governor was too much. Sam jumped into the race. Short of funds, he ran without party backing. He made only one speech. In Texas, that was enough. His name was still magic.

The Houstons arrived in Austin in December. The governor's mansion, they found, had been stripped of furniture. The state had to spend $1,500 to make the place livable. Even then, the family was crowded into four upstairs bedrooms. A seven-foot, four-poster bed gave the new governor room to stretch out.

Despite his hopes for a quiet family life, Sam Houston could not give up his political career. In 1859, he was elected governor of Texas again. The aging politician posed for this portrait in 1855.

Sam spoke out against secession. Texas, he said, "entered not into the North, nor into the South, but into the Union." To fight the drift toward civil war, he proposed a better use of the nation's strength. The United States, Sam declared, should annex Mexico. Doing so, he said, would "improve our neighborhood." Better still, the North-South conflict would end as slavery spread south. Border raids by Mexican bandits gave added force to Sam's argument. The nation, its mind fixed on the slavery issue, ignored his plan.

The desire to be president still drove Sam. As the election year of 1860 dawned, "Houston men" rallied to his cause. Their support pleased Sam, but it was not enough. The parties met, debated, and picked other men. Calling himself the "people's candidate," Sam stayed in the race. He spoke out for Southern rights—but only within the Union. Electing Abraham Lincoln, he thundered, would lead to civil war. It was not long before Sam saw that he was hurting his own cause. Rather than split the anti-Lincoln vote, he withdrew from the race.

Lincoln won the election. As Sam had forecast, South Carolina quickly left the Union. More slave states followed. The rebels formed the Confederate States of America. Would Texas follow the same path?

Sam Houston will forever be remembered as a hero in Texas. One of the state's largest cities bears his name, and monuments to him can be found all over Texas. This statue welcomes visitors to Hermann Park in Houston, Texas.

In February 1861, delegates met in Austin. They declared that Texas was part of the Confederacy. Sam opposed the move, but he had few allies. Given a chance to vote on the issue, Texans favored secession three to one. On March 15, state officials were ordered to swear loyalty to the Confederacy.

Sam did not sleep that night. In the morning, he said, "Margaret, I will never do it." When the moment came, he was as good as his word. While his fellow officials took the oath, Sam slipped out of the room. A clerk called his name three times. Sam did not respond. Friends found him in a basement room, whittling. The convention promptly replaced him with a new governor.

Two weeks later, the Civil War began. Stooped and white-haired, Sam offered to serve with the Rebels. His offer was turned down. Sam, Jr., joined the Second Texas Volunteers. He fought bravely until he was wounded at Shiloh. The Bible in his pocket absorbed much of the bullet's impact, very likely saving his life.

By 1863, the Southern cause was failing. Sam's health was no better. In July, a cold turned into pneumonia. His breathing grew labored. Family and friends crowded close to say good-bye. On July 26, Sam spoke for the last time. "Margaret! Texas . . . Texas!" he muttered. Moments later, the hero of San Jacinto was dead.

That night, Margaret opened the family Bible. She wrote, "Died on the 26th of July 1863 Genl Sam Houston, the beloved and affectionate Husband and father, the devoted patriot, the fearless soldier—the meek and lowly Christian." She knew her man. Sam could not have asked for a more fitting epitaph.

Glossary

abolitionists—People who worked to abolish slavery in the years before the Civil War.

Alamo—A former mission in San Antonio that was fortified by rebellious Texans in February 1836.

archives—An organized collection of government papers.

bar exam—A test that law students must pass before they can become licensed attorneys.

breastworks—A defensive barricade, often chest high and made of logs.

dictator—A ruler who possesses absolute power over a country and its people.

duel—An armed combat between two people fought under strict rules.

Electoral College—Under the U.S. Constitution, the group of citizens chosen by voters in each state to formally elect the president of the United States.

ensign—In the U.S. Army of the early 1800s, ensigns were the army's lowest-ranking officers.

Fugitive Slave Law—A pre-Civil War law that required the return of runaway slaves to their owners.

Know-Nothings—A popular name for members of the American party of the mid-1800s.

lacrosse—A fast-moving outdoor sport based on a traditional American Indian ball game.

militia—Part-time soldiers who are called to duty in times of emergency. Today, each state maintains a militia known as the National Guard.

musket ball—The round iron shot fired by a smoothbore, muzzle-loading musket.

omen—A natural event that is seen as a sign of future good or evil.

Panic of 1837—A national economic depression that was triggered by bank failures.

plantation—In the era before the Civil War, a large farm worked by slaves.

secede—To withdraw from a political alliance. The Civil War began after Southern states seceded from the United States in 1860–1861.

siege—An attack on a town or fortress that traps the defenders within their fortified positions.

Spanish moss—A parasitic growth that hangs from the branches of trees in long, matted clusters.

statesman—A political leader who puts service to country above party loyalties.

Texas Rangers—A force of mounted police organized in the 1800s to keep order on the Texas frontier.

Further Reading

Books

Caravantes, Peggy. *An American in Texas: The Story of Sam Houston.* Greensboro, N.C.: Morgan Reynolds Publishing, 2004.

Gregson, Susan R. *Sam Houston: Texas Hero.* Minneapolis, Minn.: Compass Point Books, 2006.

Mountjoy, Shane. *The Alamo: The Battle for Texas.* New York: Chelsea House Publishers, 2009.

Wade, Mary Dodson. *Sam Houston: I am Houston.* Houston, Tex.: Bright Sky Press, 2009.

Worth, Richard. *The Texas War of Independence: The 1800s.* New York: Marshall Cavendish Benchmark, 2008.

Internet Addresses

PBS—New Perspectives on the West: Sam Houston
<http://www.pbs.org/weta/thewest/people/d_h/houston.htm>

Sam Houston State University: Sam Houston Biography
<http://www.shsu.edu/~pin_www/samhouston/>

The Sam Houston Memorial Museum
<http://www.shsu.edu/~smm_www/>

Index